CW00890117

LINES FOR ALL OCCASIONS

Insults & Comebacks

KNOCK
KNOCK®
VENICE, CALIFORNIA

Created and published by Knock Knock
Distributed by Who's There, Inc.
Venice, CA 90291
knockknockstuff.com

© 2008 Who's There, Inc.
All rights reserved
Knock Knock is a trademark of Who's There, Inc.
Made in China

No part of this product may be used or repro-
duced in any manner whatsoever without prior
written permission from the publisher, except in
the case of brief quotations embodied in critical
articles and reviews. For information, address
Knock Knock.

This book is a work of humor meant solely for
entertainment purposes. Actually utilizing the
lines contained herein may be illegal or lead to
bodily injury. The publisher and anyone associated
with the production of this book do not advocate
breaking the law. In no event will Knock Knock be
liable to any reader for any damages, including
direct, indirect, incidental, special, consequential,
or punitive arising out of or in connection with the
use of the lines contained in this book. So there.

Every reasonable attempt has been made to
identify owners of copyright. Errors or omissions
will be corrected in subsequent editions.

Where specific company, product, and brand
names are cited, copyright and trademarks
associated with these names are property of
their respective owners.

ISBN: 978-160106058-7
UPC: 825703-50108-7

Contents

"I'm sorry, I don't speak skank."

Introduction

PREPARING TO UNLEASH THE BEAST

Whether you're teeming with frustration, overwhelmed with envy, or just plain in the mood, there are unlimited reasons to fire off an insult. From four-letter words to long-winded diatribes, backhanded compliments to in-your-face jeers, sometimes you've got to say what's really on your mind. The personal benefits of releasing such negative energy far outweigh someone else's hurt feelings. You'll feel empowered, in control, and generally better about yourself by taking down those around you. In today's world, niceness is overrated.

Philosophers understand that the pleasure of a skillfully delivered insult—and the frequently ensuing amusement—comes from the enjoyment of contrasting our own superiority with the foibles of others. Thomas Hobbes noted that "the passion of laughter is nothing else but sudden glory arising from some sudden conception of some eminency in ourselves, by comparison with the infirmity of others." Taking the comedic and insulting upper hand is an age-old form of dominance, and whether you are an insult's progenitor or have occasion to return one with a stinging comeback, delivering the right zingers will keep you at the top of the power hierarchy.

French philosopher Henri Bergson argued that comedy has a corrective purpose, pulling its target back into cultural conformity. Indeed, everyone benefits from constructive criticism. Your truth-telling statements may sting, but they also might do their recipients a favor, perhaps even inspiring a life change—a haircut, a trip to the library, or some serious counseling. We're surrounded by the ugly and the smelly, the crotchety and the immature, the stupid and the pretentious, and someone's got to take the initiative to tell it like it is.

If you're at a loss for what to insult, just remember the theory of relativity. Relatively speaking, someone

is always fatter or skinnier, older
or younger—even if only by a few
ounces or days. If they're more
stupid than you, pick on their intelligence. If they're smarter, mock
their arrogance. If they're mean,
impugn their character. If, on the
other hand, you find yourself at
the receiving end of a disparag-
ing remark, you'll find the chapter
on comebacks useful, an array of
witty ripostes for every occasion.

When selecting your words, think
about the lines that best reflect your
personality, intention, and desired
outcome. Direct or slow-burning?
Humorous or heinous? Ending or
provoking a battle? Also consider
your relationship to the insultee
and the severity of the offense. Are
you faced with an obnoxious driver,
a reckless asshole with no regard

for others? Or are you combating a friend who desperately needs encouragement to get in the shower? In addition, be sure to plan your delivery. Panache and confidence will help take the wind out of your opponents and garner the respect and admiration of others. Finally, whatever your purpose, always be sure to get in the last word.

Despite the age-old saying that "words will never hurt me," we all know that a biting comment can be a devastatingly effective slap in the face. It's not easy being mean, but *Insults and Comebacks for All Occasions* will increase your self-assurance and establish your superiority. By attacking those who need to be knocked down a peg, you'll make the world a better place one moron at a time. Bring it on!

LOOKS

When it's only skin deep

IN TODAY'S LOOKS-DRIVEN SOC-
iety, attacking people for superficial
characteristics is one of the most
effective ways to deliver a painful
insult. What's the worst thing you
can say to somebody these days? It's
not telling them that they're unkind
or lack integrity—it's "You're fat."

If you have difficulty coming to
terms with your desire to condemn

You Ain't Got No Alibi

Use caution when insulting an employee's appearance. Policies citing "community standards" of attractiveness have long been legally tolerated. However, in 2005, as part of the *Yanowitz v. L'Oréal* decision, the California Supreme Court ruled that "[Firing] a female employee for failing to meet a male executive's personal standards for sexual desirability is sex discrimination." Avoid statements such as the L'Oréal man's demand: "Get me somebody hot."

someone's appearance, remember that the ugly are polluting our environment with their toxic looks and smells—whether they are misshapen, fat, skinny, short, unhygienic, or out of style. The $160 billion-a-year global industry catering to looks—from makeup to cosmetic surgery—suggests how forceful these insults will be.

You can also pat yourself on the back for simultaneously putting someone down and accomplishing a greater good. If a friend has spinach in her teeth, you tell her, saving her from further embarrassment. The same is true if she has a gigantic nose, fat ass, flat chest, or camel toe. The sooner you inform her of her flaw, the sooner she can fix it—and that's one fewer visible (or odoriferous) offense in this world.

Don't hold back if *you* have physical imperfections, but do brush up on your comebacks—just in case. Whether or not you're supermodel caliber, the beauty of a looks-based attack is not only its efficacy, it's also the self-esteem boost that comes from taking someone down because they're different from you.

Ugly

Oh, my God! You look terrible!
Have you been sick?

Your face was made for radio.

You're dark and handsome.
When it's dark, you're handsome.

Your timeless beauty would
be enhanced by a burka.

I've had a lot to drink, and
you still don't look good.

You have such a striking face. Tell me,
how many times were you struck there?

Guess what—I've nominated you
for *Extreme Makeover* and *What Not to
Wear*, and they're fighting over you!

A good plastic surgeon could fix that.

It's too bad your hot body doesn't
make up for that nose.

Ah, I understand—you fell out
of the ugly tree and hit every
branch on the way down.

Can I borrow your face for a few
days? My ass is going on holiday.

You've got that faraway look. The
farther away I get, the better you look.

If I throw a stick, will you chase it?

Let me guess: you're the kid who made
a silly face and it stayed that way.

It's okay to be ugly, but
aren't you overdoing it?

You have such an exotic look.

You have such great hair.

You have such a great personality.

Fat

Congratulations! What's your due date?

Now that food has replaced
sex in your life, you can't even
get into your *own* pants.

Go ahead and pull up a sofa.

You must have to roll over more than
a few times to get an even tan.

Last time you were at the
beach Greenpeace tried to drag
you back in the water.

That color really complements
your stretch marks.

If you weighed five more pounds,
you could get group insurance.

I remember you when you
only had one chin.

On a scale of 1 to 10, you're a 747.

Ugly: The New Pretty?

If you want to insult someone by targeting their
looks, determine first whether you're address-
ing an ugliness competitor; if so, you may not
cause offense. Annual contests for ugliest dog
and homeliest baby draw large numbers of
contestants eager for fame and cash prizes.
In 2003, China held a Miss Ugly pageant one
week before hosting the Miss World competi-
tion. In addition to the coveted title, the winner
received $16,000 worth of plastic surgery.

Do you beep when you back up?

———•———

You may not be good at losing
weight, but you seem to be
pretty good at finding it.

———•———

When you go to a restaurant, you don't
get a menu—you get an estimate.

———•———

Your favorite food must be seconds.

———•———

Lycra really should come
with a warning label.

———•———

The only thing you can fit into at
the Gap is the dressing rooms.

———•———

I'd like to tell you about a little
something we call a gym.

———•———

I feel honored to have witnessed
your continual growth.

You have real presence.

As a matter of fact, you *do* look fat in those pants.

You have such a pretty face.

Skinny

Have you recently been on chemo?

Do you know where I can score some coke?

Heroin chic is so last millennium.

Lollipop head is *not* a sexual practice.

It's okay, eating disorders are very popular these days.

Backhanded Compliment

Some of the most effective insults come in the form of compliments. The recipient will first be flattered, then insulted—a deft one-two punch. Comments such as "You've lost so much weight!" and "Your hair looks prettier today!" sound like praise, but the insult ("You were so fat!" and "Your hair usually looks awful!") lurks just below the surface. These Trojan horse insults appear harmless but will have the desired effect nonetheless.

For God's sake, eat a sandwich.

Oh, I didn't see you—
you were turned sideways.

Did you ever have boobs?

If you were drowning, I'd
totally toss you a Cheerio.

I've never been attracted to the
twelve-year-old-boy look.

⋅•⋅

What size is less than zero?

⋅•⋅

You must use a Band-Aid as a maxi
pad and Chapstick for deodorant.

⋅•⋅

Yellow makes you look
like a no. 2 pencil.

⋅•⋅

You don't even weigh
enough to give blood.

⋅•⋅

Bitch!

Short

Are you what they call a little person?

⋅•⋅

You're so short your hair
smells like feet.

In your driver's license photo,
you can see your whole body.

———•◦•———

When it rains, are you always
the last one to know?

———•◦•———

Thank goodness you don't
have as far to fall.

———•◦•———

To qualify for a Napoleon complex,
you'd need to grow six inches.

———•◦•———

I hope you're well compensated elsewhere.

———•◦•———

At least you have big *hands*.

———•◦•———

I bet you can give blow jobs standing up.

———•◦•———

Look—a mini-me!

———•◦•———

It's all the same when you're horizontal.

Aren't you a model?
I saw you on a trophy.

———

You still use a booster seat.

———

They make man-heels nowadays.

———

My neck hurts from insulting you.

Poor Hygiene

May I suggest some manscaping?

———

I have two words for you:
personal grooming.

———

Nice cologne.
Must you marinate in it?

———

Just because you can't
smell it doesn't mean the rest
of us aren't suffering.

Using deodorant is *not* the
same as taking a shower.

———•———

It wouldn't be so bad if your
personal scent wasn't so personal.

———•———

Is it raining outside, or are
you just really sweaty?

———•———

Actually, the unibrow
look was never in.

———•———

You have beautiful hair—coming
from your nostrils and ears.

———•———

Are you going for the hippie look?

———•———

You must be a feminist.

———•———

I never used to floss until I realized
how much your breath smelled.

May I offer you a mint?

―――・―――

Actually, I just can't get past that
giant zit on your forehead.

―――・―――

Looking at you, I'm not really
in the mood for pepperoni.

―――・―――

Do me a favor, and go through
the car wash—*without* your car.

Tip: Insulting Gifts

Not all insults are verbal. Why not present a
hygiene-challenged friend with a personal-
care gift? Subtle Butt is a disposable stick-on
pad that neutralizes flatulence. Ear Scope,
a small camera, allows one to view earwax
excavation. For a more intimate insult, buy
the Weener Kleener, a donut-shaped personal
soap product, or the Biffy Squirt Travel Bidet.
Finally, go mundane with perfume, breath
mints, or deodorant.

Are you on the European laundry plan?

Are you French?

Style

It must be nice not to need a helmet
when you ride motorcycles.

The eighties called—they
want their wardrobe back.

Whatever kind of look you
were going for, you missed.

You look like shit.
Is that the style now?

You look cheap—was that the point?

You could be charged with
excessive use of denim.

Your ensemble does a terrific job
of maximizing your flaws.

———•••———

I'm sure that would look
good on someone.

———•••———

With your talent for matching,
you should get a job with Garanimals.

———•••———

Is that fabric fire retardant?

———•••———

Kudos on that camel toe.

———•••———

Very classy: visible thong
and plumber's crack.

———•••———

When you pull your pants up like
that, I can see your manhood.

———•••———

We've taken a vote:
you're trying too hard.

THE YOUNG
AND THE OLD

When it's more than a number

IN THE DOCUMENTARY *THE History of the Joke*, comedian Kathleen Madigan says audiences are almost universally willing to accept jokes about age (vs. race or sex, for example). "For one thing, it's a common trait," states Madigan. "We're all going to get old sometime." The fact that there are always going to be elderly people around means that there's endless

Don't Get No Respect

It used to be that elders were revered for their lifetime store of knowledge and wisdom. Fortunately, that's no longer the case, and old people are now acceptable targets for mockery. In explaining this shift, researchers have cited less traditional family structures, geographically spread-out families, popular culture's youth worship, parental indulgence, and generational selfishness. So, feel free to proceed with your ageist comments.

fodder for insults for the doddering. While perhaps the universality of the experience means the put-downs will be less painful than some of the other insult categories, they're still effective enough to keep in your arsenal of venom. Fortunately, culturally diminishing respect for elders means we're no longer socially prohibited from slamming seniors—whether for their aging minds, sagging bodies, or sad social lives.

It's also important to put uppity young 'uns in their place. Callow youth think they know everything. This is not only annoying, it's a cry for retribution. How else will the know-it-all young come to understand their ignorance and, most important, their place? Make sure these sophomoric upstarts realize the advantages of your experience and wisdom and point out their naiveté at every opportunity.

Those who think young stay young at heart. What could keep you feeling more youthful than the smug satisfaction and gleeful hilarity that comes from insulting others for their age, young or old?

Out of Touch

It's time to start acting
your age—old.

Is your memory in black and white?

It may seem like yesterday to
you, but it was decades ago.

You're so over the hill, you
don't remember crossing it.

You're so old, you think a
BlackBerry is a fruit.

You're so old, you think the
Internet is a series of tubes.

You're so old, you
actually think I should
focus on earning a living.

You're so old, you still get
dressed up when you fly.

———•—•———

You're so old, you leave notes
to remind yourself to pee.

———•—•———

You're so old, when you lie about
your age you tell the truth.

———•—•———

Yes, I've heard that story
before. An hour ago.

———•—•———

You know *so* much. Too bad you
don't remember anything.

———•—•———

It must be hard to be nostalgic when
you have no memory of your past.

———•—•———

Congratulations on reaching
your second childhood!

———•—•———

U R 2 old.

Aging Bodies

Your biological clock
has stopped ticking.

The sell-by date on your
eggs is about to expire.

For some people, forty is the
new twenty-nine, but I don't
think you can pull that off.

Does it take you twice as long
to look half as good?

The good news is you look like
you should be respected; the
bad news is you're not.

Why doesn't your face move?

It may be too late for Botox.

Poor thing—wrinkles *and* acne!

————————

You look like a million bucks—
all green and wrinkled.

————————

You should show off your elbows more—
they're the smoothest part of your body.

————————

What's left of your hair
is getting so gray!

Youth: Wasted on the Old

The booming youth-maintenance market is
a testament of age insults. If aging weren't
a sensitive topic, the United States wouldn't
have logged over 11 million cosmetic proce-
dures in 2007, with Botox leading the way. If
you believe the pharmaceutical commercials,
as many as 30 million older American men
suffer from erectile dysfunction. When people
freeze their faces and their penises to freeze
time, there's plenty to laugh about.

35

What a double whammy to say goodbye
to both your hipness *and* your hip.

———•◦•———

The only thing you should
exercise is caution.

———•◦•———

It takes you longer to rest
than it did to get tired.

———•◦•———

At least your failing eyes will keep you
from seeing the rest of your failing body.

———•◦•———

Your medical history reads
like *The Merck Manual.*

———•◦•———

Your conversation sounds
like *The Merck Manual.*

———•◦•———

You must really identify with
prescription drug commercials.

———•◦•———

You're so old, you fart dust.

Aging Social Lives

It's time you stop looking for Mr. Right
and start looking for Mr. Right Now.

———•—•———

After painting the town red,
do you have to rest awhile before
applying a second coat?

———•—•———

It must get heavy carrying
around that generation gap.

———•—•———

That menoPorsche is such a cliché.

———•—•———

If this is your midlife crisis, I guess
you're planning to live to 120.

———•—•———

When you're on vacation, your energy
runs out before your money does.

———•—•———

Do you burn the midnight
oil until 9 PM?

Fight the Power

By preparing yourself to taunt the elderly, you're planning for the future. Thanks to the large baby boomer population and increased life expectancy, the number of maturing seniors (age fifty-five and older) in the United States will increase over 40 percent by 2020; worldwide, the number is expected to top one billion by 2030. Given that this expanding demographic will strain the economy and families alike, the insults will be well deserved.

Now that you're old enough to watch your step, you're too old to go anywhere.

Your idea of happy hour is a nap.

Your little black book only contains names ending in MD.

You can't get it up—you can't even get *up*.

I'd ask you to go upstairs and make
love to me, but I don't think you're
young enough to do either.

———•———

To someone your age,
"getting lucky" means finding
your car in the parking lot.

———•———

You're so old, your idea of oral
sex is talking about it.

———•———

You get tired wrestling with temptation.

———•———

You still watch the nightly news.

Ancient History

Your social security number
must be in the single digits.

———•———

They've asked you to be on *Antiques
Roadshow*—to be appraised.

I was at the ancient history museum
today and thought of you.

———•·•———

When you were in school,
history was called "current events."

———•·•———

When you were in school,
evolution hadn't happened yet.

———•·•———

When you were born,
the Dead Sea was just sick.

———•·•———

Weren't you a waiter
at the Last Supper?

———•·•———

Does *Jurassic Park* bring back memories?

———•·•———

You're so old, the candles
cost more than the cake.

———•·•———

You're so old, you should buy
calendars one month at a time.

I wish I'd known you
when you were alive.

———•◦•———

If I told you to act your age, you'd die.

Callow Youth

You remind me of when
I was young and clueless.

———•◦•———

You still think a paycheck is what
you spend on your wardrobe.

———•◦•———

You still think you'll have
that body forever.

———•◦•———

You still think you can be anything
you want—and get paid for it.

———•◦•———

You still think the world owes you.

———•◦•———

You still think you can change the world.

You still think you can change him.

———•◦•———

You still think your dreams
will come true.

———•◦•———

You still think you can have it all.

———•◦•———

You still think you're hot shit.

———•◦•———

You still think you know everything.

———•◦•———

You're so young, you think
you deserve promotions and
raises without hard work.

———•◦•———

You're so young, you think
people other than your parents
will believe you're special.

———•◦•———

You're so young, you don't know
you need to dial 1 before a long-
distance call on a landline.

Your lack of experience is matched
only by your surplus of ego.

⸺⸻⸺

Your youthful idealism
makes me want to puke.

⸺⸻⸺

You should have grown
out of that by now.

⸺⸻⸺

Grow up!

Tip: Don't Give Them Tips

It's easy to get irritated when talking to the
young: they're naive, immature, idealistic
know-it-alls. Don't ever try to share your wisdom; they'll never grasp it, and their quick wit
may get the best of you, as in this fifth-century-
BC exchange between uncle and nephew:

Pericles: "When I was your age, Alcibiades,
I talked just the way you are now talking."

Alcibiades: "If only I had known you,
Pericles, when you were at your best."

BRAINS

When they just don't get it

YOU'VE ALREADY PROVEN YOUR intelligence by choosing to utilize this compendium of insults. Now, it's time to take down the lesser beings around you. Whether they're dumber than a doorknob, emotionally challenged, or even too smart for their own good, you shouldn't have to put up with their idiocy, because you now have the skill and wit to put them in their place.

Survival of the Fittest

The Darwin Awards recognize and commemorate those whose extreme stupidity kills them, thus removing them from the gene pool. One award winner, a Polish farmer, chopped off his own head with a chain saw during a drunken game of macho one-upmanship. Two college students were recognized for crawling into a giant helium advertising balloon to get high; due to their failure to remember the human need for oxygen, they suffocated.

Morons lurk everywhere. Idiot drivers, incompetent coworkers, basket-case friends, socially inept experts—you are surrounded. And no doubt you're sick of it. Your victim's level of intelligence or education is actually immaterial, because your insult will be a reaction to an unbelievably imbecilic moment or to your target's overall ineptitude.

For those who are truly stupid,
keep it simple. If they're not book
smart, prey on their insecurities by
using big words. For the talent-free,
let them know that their cooking
sucks, they can't write, or they're
just plain mediocre. If they're
emotionally weak-minded—those
who may seem otherwise intel-
ligent but who fall again and again
into destructive patterns—be
sure to point this out when it
arises. Finally, a smarty-pants
is just as annoying as a dimwit.
Remember that "pretentious"
comes from the root for "pretend":
these blowhards need to be taken
down, their bombast exposed.

With this book, you've got the
smarts to combat both boneheads
and braggarts. Get out there
and cut them off at the knees.

Just Plain Stupid

I don't know what makes you
so dumb, but it really works.

If brains were taxed,
you'd get a rebate.

If you spoke your mind,
you'd be speechless.

Don't get lost in thought—
it's unfamiliar territory.

Don't let your mind wander—
it's too little to be let out alone.

You're so dumb, blondes
tell jokes about *you*.

You're so dumb, your dog
teaches *you* tricks.

You're so dumb, you sold
your car for gas money.

You're so dumb, you think a lawsuit
is something you wear to court.

If you were any smarter,
I could teach you to fetch.

Brains aren't everything. In fact,
in your case they're nothing.

Ever wonder what life would have been
like if you'd had enough oxygen at birth?

If what you don't know can't hurt
you, you're practically invulnerable.

Most people live and learn. You just live.

You'd need twice as much
sense to be a half-wit.

You're like one of those idiot savants,
except without the "savant" part.

Did you take the short bus to school?

Ignorance can be cured. Stupid is forever.

Not Book Smart

I wish I were as smart as
you think you are.

If you can't pronounce it, don't say it.

I'm sorry—I didn't mean to
use so many syllables.

Really? You "could care less?"

Good thing you're not letting
your education get in the
way of your ignorance.

You really earned that BS
degree, didn't you?

———•◦•———

Don't let the facts get in the
way of your opinions.

———•◦•———

Where'd you hear that—on a blog?

———•◦•———

You should get a refund on
that college education.

Dumb to the Roots

The time-honored "dumb blonde" joke
dates to the 1925 publication of Anita Loos's
novel *Gentlemen Prefer Blondes*. The book
showcased Lorelei Lee, a ditzy, gold-digging
blonde—who was actually pretty smart. After
a lesser-known 1928 film version, Lorelei was,
of course, famously played by Marilyn Monroe
in 1953. Blondes make great targets for insults
because they're often too dumb to realize
they're being put down—see how easy it is?

Congratulations on barely graduating.

———•◦•———

I'd love to rip apart the shallow
logic you call a point, but the
Americans with Disabilities Act
prohibits picking on the retarded.

———•◦•———

I'd like to insult you, but
you wouldn't get it.

Lacking in Skills

Your mediocrity is unparalleled.

———•◦•———

Oh, I'm sorry—I didn't realize
I was supposed to laugh.

———•◦•———

For some, following a recipe is just hard.

———•◦•———

Spell-check was invented for people
like you. Unfortunately, you're the
least likely to actually use it.

It's not the technology—it's you.

—•—

When the computer says "Press
any key to continue," you're not
supposed to press the "Any" key.

—•—

The fact that no one understands
you doesn't mean you're an artist.

—•—

One of the defining characteristics
of writers is the fact that they write.

—•—

You're the only one who
believes in your talent.

—•—

Talking about it and doing it are two
very different things. At least you
excel at something: talking about it.

—•—

You throw like a girl who can't throw.

—•—

Don't quit your day job.

53

So Many Stupid People

According to the U.S. Department of Education, the high school graduation rate is about 88 percent. A new study by economists James Heckman and Paul LaFontaine, however, indicates a substantially lower—and declining—rate. Another source claims that every year 1.2 million students fail to graduate on time. Whatever the statistics, one thing's for sure: idiots abound. As George W. Bush once asked, "Is our children learning?"

The Classic: One Short, Two Shy

You're one banana short of a fruit salad.

You're one sentence short of a paragraph.

You're two sheep short of a sweater.

You're a couple of knights
short of a Crusade.

You're a few beers short of a six-pack.

You're a few birds shy of a flock.

You're a few clowns short of a circus.

You're a few Bradys short of a bunch.

You're a few eggs short of a dozen.

You're a few feet short of the runway.

You're a few peas short of a pod.

You're a few rungs short of a ladder.

You're a few french fries
short of a Happy Meal.

You're a few sandwiches short of a picnic.

Emotionally Retarded

Baggage is one thing; steamer
trunks are another.

When something happens to *you*
over and over again, what do you
think is the common denominator?

If you pay attention, you can
tell when people aren't interested
in what you have to say.

It's not a badge of honor always to
be the last person at the party.

Let me guess, you're in love—again.

You just think you're in love.

You would think being married
four times was enough.

You're smart, funny,
and pretty, and you have
terrible taste in men.

—·•·—

You're smart, funny,
and handsome, and you have
terrible taste in women.

—·•·—

Don't you think you're taking
this a little bit too hard?

—·•·—

Don't you think you're taking
this a little bit too well?

—·•·—

What did you expect?

—·•·—

Get ahold of yourself.

—·•·—

Get over it already.

—·•·—

Can't you see the pattern here?

Smarty-Pants

It's lonely at the top, isn't it?

———◦•◦———

Peppering your speech with foreign
phrases does not endear you to others.

———◦•◦———

Yes, you have a huge vocabulary,
but what good is it if no
one understands you?

———◦•◦———

You're just not user-friendly.

———◦•◦———

You're what they call "book
smart," and not in a good way.

———◦•◦———

Making other people feel stupid
doesn't make you seem smarter.

———◦•◦———

If you were as smart as you think
you are, you'd realize you come
off like a pretentious asshole.

Clearly you've chosen knowing
everything over having friends.

———◦✦◦———

Why don't you just join
Mensa and call it a day?

———◦✦◦———

Differential equations
just aren't sexy.

———◦✦◦———

Is it worth it?

Tip: Techie Taxonomy

When insulting a smarty-pants, be sure to use
the correct jargon. On the Internet (natch), the
distinctions between nerds, geeks, dweebs,
and dorks are minutely parsed. A nerd is an
iconoclast with eclectic intellectual interests,
while a geek is a nerd who specializes in an
area of extreme passion; though socially outside the mainstream, in the computer age both
are considered somewhat cool. Dweebs and
dorks, however, are still losers, so fire away.

CHARACTER

When they totally suck

WHEN WE CONTEMPLATE CHAR-
acter, we think of traits such as
morality, integrity, humaneness,
maturity, honesty, and kindness.
As evidenced by chapter 1, our
society values beauty and celebrity
far more than the deeper virtues,
but there's still much to target in a
character-based attack. And with
fewer people exhibiting sound
character these days, there are

You're Worse Than...

Compare the assholes and bitches in your life to Leona Helmsley, the "Queen of Mean." Among the New York hotel tycoon's many infamous actions, she evicted her newly widowed daughter-in-law and grandson and sued them for their inheritance; forced her employees to crawl and beg; and stated "Only little people pay taxes" before being convicted of tax fraud. Upon her death, she left $12 million to her dog—and nothing to two grandchildren.

plenty of individuals for whom these insults will prove handy.

It is said that the flaws we hate the most in others are the flaws we ourselves possess, so go right ahead and condemn people for things you yourself do. If you are any of the types addressed in this chapter— assholes, bitches, egotists, attitude givers, nutjobs, freaks, liars, cheats, sluts, man-whores, losers, and bores—your vast insight will give you a clear path to takedown.

If you're a decent, ethical person, you'll need this chapter's guidance all the more, because your moral compass won't allow you to come up with appropriate attacks. While you may feel initially guilty about going on the offensive, be confident in your approach and message—chances are you're not the only one your target aggravates.

Whether you are a good or bad person, if you encounter someone with multiple contemptible characteristics, go for the combo approach: choose insults from the various categories to concoct a nuclear affront, then rest assured that the world will be grateful.

Assholes and Bitches

If I wanted to hear from
an asshole, I'd fart.

If I'd wanted a bitch,
I would've gotten a dog.

Do you have to work
that hard to be a jerk, or does
it just come naturally?

You used to be arrogant and
obnoxious. Now you're the
opposite—obnoxious and arrogant.

You're not yourself today!
I noticed the improvement immediately.

Since your personality acts as a
birth control device, you must
save lots of money on condoms.

When someone first meets you, they
don't like you. But when they get to
know you better, they hate you.

———•—•———

I don't think you're an asshole,
but I seem to be in the minority.

———•—•———

You're not even *beneath* my contempt.

———•—•———

You're the reason God created
the middle finger.

———•—•———

Your father should have pulled out.

———•—•———

It must be that time of the month.

———•—•———

Men have that time of the month, too.

———•—•———

When you take Viagra,
do you get taller?

When people say you're the perfect
jerk, I tell them you're not perfect,
but you're doing all right.

You should come with a warning label.

Egos and Attitudes

Jesus may love you, but everybody
else thinks you're an ass.

I bet that attitude of yours was
really cool back in high school.

There's Mr. Right,
there's Mr. Wrong, and then
there's you—Mr. Never Wrong.

Are you still paying off your
student loans to poseur school?

I know you're self-made.
It's big of you to take the blame!

You're such a smart-ass I bet you could sit on a carton of ice cream and tell what flavor it is.

———•◦•———

I'm impressed. I've never met someone with such a small mind inside such a big head before.

———•◦•———

What exactly does your big head compensate for?

Silent but Deadly

Anthropologists estimate that over 90 percent of communication is nonverbal. Whatever the situation, the lines in this book can, therefore, take you only so far. For example, if you want to ding someone lightly, smile when you deliver your insult. If the infraction is dire, roll your eyes and snort in disgust. Stand-alone signs such as the middle finger, up yours (fist to upward-bending inner elbow), or chin flick will always help you get the last nonword in.

You're even more self-absorbed
than I am; it would never work.

Yes, the cream rises to the
top, but so does the scum.

It'll be a lonely day when
all you have to keep you
company is your own ego.

I'm so jealous that you finally found
your true love. Unfortunately, they
haven't legalized self-marriage yet.

It's hard to get over yourself, isn't it?

Nutjobs and Freaks

I'm guessing you haven't
been diagnosed yet.

Your personality's split so many ways
you go alone for group therapy.

Who am I talking to today?

You might want to go back
home to take your meds.

Have you thought about
upping the dosage?

It's supposed to be *better* living
through modern chemistry.

You're so crazy, there
wouldn't even be a trial.

Your mind isn't just
twisted—it's sprained.

As an outsider, what do you
think of the human race?

You're not even half-baked—
you're just plain raw.

69

Tip: Gaslighting

When dealing with someone who's a little loony, don't just *call* him crazy—*make* him crazy, then follow up by insulting his sanity. The classic 1944 thriller *Gaslight* depicts a woman tricked into thinking she's going mad. Her husband moves objects and dims the gaslights and then denies that anything is happening—hence the term "gaslight," to manipulate someone's perceptions so she will believe she's losing her mind.

You must have gotten up on the wrong side of the padded room this morning.

———

Is that what a relapse looks like?

———

Let me guess—you're going to rehab to "rest."

———

I bet your therapist is publishing a paper on you.

Your baggage is so heavy you can't
even lug it onto the couch.

⸺•⸺

You put the *psycho* in *psychology*.

Liars and Cheats

You'd make a great politician.

⸺•⸺

You'd steal the straw from
your mother's kennel.

⸺•⸺

You're as good as your word,
and your vocabulary sucks.

⸺•⸺

Calling you a dirty liar would
be an insult to dirty liars.

⸺•⸺

You're so dishonest, I can't even be
sure that what you tell me are lies.

⸺•⸺

You're so full of shit, your eyes are brown.

You're so two-faced, your
spouse will be a bigamist.

Mt. Rushmore's got nothing on you.

The only difference between
you and a mosquito is that
one is a bloodsucking parasite
and the other is an insect.

I didn't get why they called it
the rat race until I met you.

Your motto is if two wrongs
don't make a right, try a third.

You have a gift for sex—
usually it's diamonds.

I'm surprised you can see past
those dollar signs in your eyes.

I can always tell when you're
lying. Your lips move.

———

Death wouldn't be that
big of a deal for you—
either way, you're lying.

———

You must get lots of exercise talking
out of both sides of your mouth.

———

Even if you make yourself
believe it, it's still a lie.

———

You lie like a rug.

Sluts and Man-Whores

You're a lot like train tracks—
you've been laid across the country.

———

Did you install that shag carpet
because it's easier to hang on to?

Your body is like a temple—
open to everyone, day or night.

———•◦•———

You're so slutty,
you take the morning-after
pill the night before.

———•◦•———

You're so slutty,
your gynecologist is on speed dial.

———•◦•———

You're so slutty,
you buy condoms at Costco.

———•◦•———

You've got so many notches on
your belt, it's falling apart.

———•◦•———

You've got standards—
nothing but women.

———•◦•———

You've got standards—
nothing but humans.

You've got standards—
nothing but mammals.

—•—

You give a whole new meaning
to the phrase "all access."

—•—

Your knees haven't touched in a decade.

—•—

One word for next time—
kneepads.

Specific Neologisms

Certain put-downs are originated by particular groups to describe unique situations. Some favorites: seagull manager (a bureaucrat who flies in, makes a lot of noise, craps all over everything, and leaves), Velcroid (someone who ghosts a celebrity in order to get into photos), 404 (clueless, from the HTML error message "404 error: File not found"), and whorganic (of or pertaining to the naturally whorish). The possibilities are endless!

At what number did you lose count?

If you were a girl, you'd be called a ho.

Losers and Bores

Your inferiority complex is fully justified.

Do you want me to accept you as you
are, or do you want me to like you?

I'm trying to imagine you
with a personality.

Anyone who told you to be yourself
couldn't have given you worse advice.

You remind me of one of those people
in school that no one remembers.

You're one bad relationship away
from having thirty cats.

You're such a loser, your imaginary
friends wouldn't hang out with you.

———•———

You're such a loser, you've got bedsores
from watching the *Survivor* marathon.

———•———

You're such a loser, when someone tells
you to get a life, you ask, "Where?"

———•———

You're so boring, you can't
even entertain a doubt.

———•———

You're better than Ambien, and cheaper.

———•———

There must be *something*
interesting about you.

———•———

You bore me, and I even enjoy
watching paint dry.

———•———

Googling you yielded no results.

COUNTER-ATTACKS

When it's time to strike back

IT'S A SAD REALITY OF LIFE THAT
you won't always be the one
delivering the insult—sometimes
others will attack you. Since you
don't know when or from where
such an assault will occur, you'll
want to be sure your defensive
game is buttoned up. As you insult
more frequently, others will begin
to admire your clever zingers.
They'll turn on you quickly, and

Avoiding the Staircase

The French expression *l'esprit de l'escalier* means "the wit of the staircase": the devastatingly witty comeback concocted *after* the confrontation, too late to deliver, on the way down the staircase. Germans have coined a similar term: *treppenwitz* (*treppen* means "stairs," *witz* means "wit"). With practice and the lines in this chapter, your goal is to preempt the staircase, issuing your scathing ripostes on point and on time.

you'd better be ready with as much wit in the return as in the serve.

Depending on your relationship with the attacker and the manner in which they attack, there are many ways to craft your response. In some instances, you'll simply want to call upon a classic—short, sharp, and direct. You can select one that's dismissive, suggesting that they are *so* not worth your time, or one that's potentially duel inciting, in which case you'll emerge as the silver-tongued victor.

For a particularly mean insult, you'll want to have an equally cutting reply. For complete idiots or the utterly demented, make sure your retort expresses just how unoriginal or nonsensical your attackers are. Or, when you've simply had enough, unleash an end-all line that will shut them up for good.

Rehearse these lines so you'll be ready for any barb hurled your way—no momentum-killing pause, no stumbling over your words, no thinking of the perfect comeback hours too late. This is your moment to shine, when you can truly put your skills to the test and leave others in your comeback wake.

Invoking the Classics

Bite me!

———•—•———

Bring it on!

———•—•———

Oh, it's *so* on.

———•—•———

Feel special now?

———•—•———

Take a chill pill.

———•—•———

Talk to the hand.

———•—•———

Talk to the booty, 'cause
the hand's off duty!

———•—•———

That's not what your
mother said last night.

———•—•———

Up your nose with a rubber hose.

It takes one to know one!

Whatever.

As if!

Am not!

I know you are, but what am I?

I'm rubber, you're glue;
whatever you say bounces off
me and sticks to you.

Sticks and stones may
break my bones, but words
will never hurt me.

Liar, liar, pants on fire!

Shut your pie hole!

Piss off.

Up yours!

Here's a quarter—
call someone who cares.

Thank you for sharing.

Get a life!

Get a sex life!

Yo' mama.

Dealing with Mean

A sharp tongue is no indication
of a keen mind.

I'm not your mother—don't yell at me.

Did your mother teach you
to treat people like that?

───•••───

It's clear from your behavior
that you must have had a
miserable childhood.

───•••───

Let's switch places: you be
funny, and I'll be an asshole.

Yo' Mama

Also known as *the dozens, capping,* and *dissing,* "yo' mama" has evolved into a call-and-response competitive art form. Insult matches date at least to the eighth century, when Arab poets traded barbs in the town square, collected as *Al-Naqa'id.* And in the Middle Ages, Scots verbally abused one another in flyting contests. Today, "mama" insults target obesity, appearance, and stupidity. As a comeback, simply replying "Yo' mama" is a classic.

I will always cherish the initial
misconceptions I had about you.

———•———

I'm only interested in the
opinions of people I respect.

———•———

I may be fat, but you're ugly,
and I can always diet.

———•———

I may be ignorant, but you're
stupid, and I can always study.

———•———

I may be immature, but you're
old, and I can always grow up.

———•———

I may be a bitch,
but you're an asshole,
and I can always get walked.

———•———

People treat others the way
they feel about themselves—
it must be hard to be you.

Someday you'll find out the truth: karma's a bitch.

Careful, there—if the redness in your face is any indication, your blood pressure's on the rise.

You don't want to blow a gasket, because I'm not a mechanic.

Wow, you're as mean as everybody says you are.

Responding to Idiots

Wow, it must have hurt when your daddy dropped you.

Did you eat lots of paste as a kid?

Does your stream of consciousness have any fish in it?

The International Hater

When responding to an insult from an idiot, try using another language to make your opponent feel even more stupid than he or she may actually be. Try "idiot" in Finnish (*tampio*), Portuguese (*abestado*), Hawaiian (*hupo*), Tagalog (*tanga*), French (*connard*), or Russian (*слабоумный*). Consult translation dictionaries for more variations on the theme, or use sign language: make a fist and strike your forehead as though knocking sense into it.

Do you do children's parties?

I can see your point, but
I still think you're an idiot.

The next time I need an
unsolicited and uninformed
opinion, I'll know where to go.

That insult is older than your underwear.

That insult is staler than your breath.

That insult was out of date
when Adam used it on Eve.

It must be nice to be free of
the burden of intelligence.

If I agreed with you,
we'd both be wrong.

You have nothing to say,
but you say it so loudly.

Your lips are moving,
but nothing's coming out.

Where'd you find that phrase?
Online?

I'm blonde. What's your excuse?

Calling It Crazy

Are you in therapy for that?

———•———

You might want to cut back on the sugar.

———•———

It's nice to meet an alcoholic who
doesn't want to remain anonymous.

———•———

I'm sorry, I don't speak in tongues.

———•———

I don't know what your problem is,
but I'll bet it's hard to pronounce.

———•———

My mother told me not to
speak to strange people.

———•———

I see you've set aside this special time
to humiliate yourself in public.

———•———

Cancel my subscription—
I can't deal with your issues.

Any resemblance between your reality
and mine is strictly coincidental.

———•◦•———

Did you not get enough
attention at home?

———•◦•———

They have a special place
for people like you.

———•◦•———

You put the *k* in *crazy.*

———•◦•———

Are you for real?

Shutting Them Up

I'm visualizing duct tape
over your mouth.

———•◦•———

How about a little less talk
and a little more shut-the-hell-up?

———•◦•———

I don't like you—and I always will.

Save your breath. You'll need
it to blow up your date.

———•———

I'm busy now. Can I ignore
you some other time?

———•———

Don't bother me; I'm living
happily ever after.

———•———

There's a game you might enjoy:
it's called hide and go screw yourself.

———•———

I don't mind your talking
as long as you don't mind
my not listening.

———•———

I'd like to give you a
going-away present, but you
have to do your part.

———•———

I'd like to help you out.
Which way did you come in?

If I promise to miss you,
will you go away?

You've obviously mistaken me
for someone who gives a shit.

Is that the best you've got?

Why are you even talking?

Tip: Crafting a Comeback

To deliver stellar comebacks, take a few point-
ers from improv performers, for whom a classic
pitfall is thinking about their response rather
than listening to their partners. Until it's time
for you to reply, focus carefully on your opponent's words. Then come from a place of "Yes,
and . . ." rather than "No, but . . ." to help your
verbal flexibility. The skill of the comeback
is akin to martial arts—you must stay in the
moment and play off your opponent's moves.

FAMOUS LIP

When the sass has class

INSULTS AREN'T LIMITED TO LAY-
people. Well-known actors, artists,
writers, musicians, and politicians
are also deep in the game. Part of
the reason for their success is that
they know half of looking good is
making others look bad. For some,
publicly documented insults were
their original claims to fame.

Where the previous chapters
provided actual verbiage for your

The Insult Bard

Among other things, William Shakespeare has gone down in history as creator of the most original insults ever written. Try an easy-to-follow method to craft your own: first, choose a degrading adjective; next, a hyphenated, verb-derived adjective; and finally, link them with a rich noun (for example, *dumpy* plus *addle-brained* plus *sow*). Or, use a direct quote from the master (say, "poisonous bunch-back'd toad").

everyday usage, here you will find inspiration for the inevitable moments when you need to go off-script. At this point in the book, you should have a fairly solid grasp of what lines to use when. Now that you're at least at the intermediate level, you'll be even more impressed at the verbal acuity of insults that have stood

the test of time. Indeed, perhaps
the most acclaimed lines aren't
insults, but comebacks, as celebri-
ties who are able to turn an attack
into an even better affront garner
the most respect and admiration.

Hopefully this book has piqued
your interest in the insult and
comeback arts. If you want to go
further for inspiration, investigate
the words of such greats as Oscar
Wilde, Groucho Marx, Dorothy
Parker, and Mark Twain. With a
little practice, you too may be able
to conjure up insults so perfect,
so apropos, so witty, that they
live on forever not only in the
hearts and minds of those who
were lucky enough to have heard
them, but on the written page as
an example of the best of the best.

Celebs on Looks

"Prince looks like a dwarf who's been dipped in a bucket of pubic hair." —Boy George

---

"She has discovered the secret of perpetual middle age." —Oscar Levant, on Zsa Zsa Gabor

---

"His ears make him look like a taxicab with both doors open." —Howard Hughes, on Clark Gable

---

"In her last days, she resembled a spoiled pear." —Gore Vidal, on Gertrude Stein

---

"Mick Jagger is about as sexy as a pissing toad." —Truman Capote

---

"Is he just doing a bad Elvis pout, or was he born that way?" —Freddie Mercury, on Billy Idol

"She's so hairy—when she lifted up her arm I thought it was Tina Turner in her armpit." —Joan Rivers, on Madonna

---

"She had much in common with Hitler, only no mustache." —Noel Coward, on Mary Baker Eddy

---

"A woman whose face looked as if it had been made of sugar and someone licked it." —George Bernard Shaw, on Isadora Duncan

---

"His mouth is a no-go area. It's like kissing the Berlin Wall." —Helena Bonham Carter, on Woody Allen

---

"He looks as though he'd been weaned on a pickle." —Alice Roosevelt Longworth, on Calvin Coolidge

---

"I never forget a face, but in your case, I'll make an exception." —Groucho Marx, target unknown

"Do you mind if I sit back a little?
Because your breath is very bad."
—Donald Trump, to Larry King

Celebs on Brains

"He had a mind so fine that no idea could
violate it." —T. S. Eliot, on Henry James

"He has the lucidity which is the
by-product of a fundamentally
sterile mind." —Aneurin Bevan,
on Neville Chamberlain

"His mind was like a soup dish, wide and
shallow; it could hold a small amount of
nearly anything, but the slightest jarring
spilled the soup into somebody's lap."
—Irving Stone, on William
Jennings Bryan

"He can compress the most words into
the smallest idea of any man I know."
—Abraham Lincoln, target unknown

"If he were any dumber, he'd be a tree."
—Barry Goldwater, on William Scott

—————

"A genius with the IQ of a moron."
—Gore Vidal, on Andy Warhol

—————

"Logically unsound, confused, and
unprincipled, unwise to the extreme."
—Jiang Zemin, on George W. Bush

Musical Digs

Some of today's most quotable put-downs come
from popular-music lyrics. Set your insult to a
melody or beat and before long others will sing
your slur. Here are some toe-tapping favorites:
"Every time I think of you, I puke." —Eminem
• "Were you born an asshole, or did you work
at it your whole life?" —Jimmy Buffett • "I'm
so ugly, but that's okay, 'cause so are you."
—Nirvana • "Idiot wind, blowing every time
you move your mouth." —Bob Dylan

"He's a nice guy, but he played too much football with his helmet off."
—Lyndon B. Johnson, on Gerald Ford

"It's a new low for actresses when you have to wonder what's between her ears instead of her legs." —Katharine Hepburn, on Sharon Stone

---

"She's a vacuum with nipples." —Otto Preminger, on Marilyn Monroe

Celebs on Character

" . . . a swaggering, tough little slut."
—Louise Brooks, on Shirley Temple

"He's the type of man who will end up dying in his own arms." —Mamie Van Doren, on Warren Beatty

---

"Paul Newman has the attention span of a bolt of lightning." —Robert Redford

"Good taste would likely have the same
effect on Howard Stern that daylight
has on Dracula." —Ted Koppel

"I knew her before she was a virgin."
—Oscar Levant, on Doris Day

"There is absolutely nothing wrong
with Oscar Levant that a miracle
can't fix." —Alexander Woollcott

"The man was a major comedian, which
is to say that he had the compassion of
an icicle, the effrontery of a carnival shill,
and the generosity of a pawnbroker."
—S. J. Perelman, on Groucho Marx

"He was humane but not human."
—e. e. cummings, on Ezra Pound

"Always willing to lend a helping hand
to the one above him." —F. Scott
Fitzgerald, on Ernest Hemingway

Tip: Affix an Epithet

If you asked Typhoid Mary, Vlad the Impaler, or Ivan the Terrible, you'd learn that the unflattering epithet—permanently linked to one's name—is the ultimate form of offense. Many historic rulers have had to live down devastating sobriquets, such as Ethelred the Unready, Halfdan the Mild, Charles the Bald, and Ivailo the Cabbage. Come up with a descriptive epithet, repeat it frequently, and hope your enemy will be saddled with it forever!

"He is limp and damp and milder than the breath of a cow." —Virginia Woolf, on E. M. Forster

---

"Henry James was one of the nicest old ladies I ever met." —William Faulkner

---

"He is the same old sausage, fizzing and sputtering in his own grease." —Henry James, on Thomas Carlyle

"I loathe you. You revolt me stewing
in your consumption . . . you are a
loathsome reptile—I hope you die."
—D. H. Lawrence, to Katherine Mansfield

"For years I've regarded [his] very
existence as a monument to all the
rancid genes and broken chromosomes
that corrupt the possibilities of
the American Dream; he was a foul
caricature of himself, a man with no soul,
no inner convictions, with the integrity
of a hyena and the style of a poison toad."
—Hunter S. Thompson, on
Richard Nixon

"He can't help it—he was born with
a silver foot in his mouth." —Ann
Richards, on George H. W. Bush

"He has no more backbone than
a chocolate éclair." —Theodore
Roosevelt, on William McKinley

"If they can make penicillin out
of moldy bread, they can sure make
something out of you."
—Muhammad Ali, to a young boxer

"What other problems do you
have besides being unemployed,
a moron, and a dork?" —John
McEnroe, to a tennis spectator

Celebs on Talent

"He bores me. He ought to have stuck
to his flying machines." —Auguste
Renoir, on Leonardo da Vinci

". . . a skillful but short-lived decorator."
—Edgar Degas, on Claude Monet

"I have tried lately to read Shakespeare,
and found it so intolerably dull that it
nauseated me." —Charles Darwin

"A hack writer . . . who tried out a few of the old proven 'sure-fire' literary skeletons with sufficient local color to intrigue the superficial and the lazy."
—William Faulkner, on Mark Twain

"An essentially private man who wished his total indifference to public notice to be universally recognized."
—Tom Stoppard, on James Joyce

"That's not writing, that's typing."
—Truman Capote, on Jack Kerouac

"*Uncle Tom's Cabin* was the first evidence to America that no hurricane can be so disastrous to a country as a ruthlessly humanitarian woman." —Sinclair Lewis, on Harriet Beecher Stowe

"He writes his plays for the ages—the ages between five and twelve." —George Nathan, on George Bernard Shaw

"She ran the whole gamut of emotions from A to B." —Dorothy Parker, on Katharine Hepburn

---

"He couldn't ad-lib a fart after a baked-bean dinner." —Johnny Carson, on Chevy Chase

---

"Wet, she's a star. Dry, she ain't." —Fanny Brice, on Esther Williams

---

"He is to acting what Liberace was to pumping iron." —Rex Reed, on Sylvester Stallone

---

"She projects the passion of a Good Humor ice cream: frozen, on a stick, and all vanilla." —Spencer Tracy, on Nancy Davis (later Nancy Reagan)

"I have more talent in my smallest fart than you have in your entire body."— Walter Matthau, to Barbra Streisand

"Her voice sounded like an eagle being goosed." —Ralph Novak, on Yoko Ono

* * *

"Michael Jackson's album was only called *Bad* because there wasn't enough room on the sleeve for *Pathetic*." —Prince

* * *

"The late Bill Nye once said, 'I have been told that Wagner's music is better than it sounds.'" —Mark Twain

Merchant of Venom

The comedian Don Rickles built his long career on the art of the insult. His equal-opportunity barbs (he mocks all races, life-styles, and religions), honed against hecklers, skillfully manage to malign without being contemptuous. In 1957, he made his mark with Frank Sinatra, a notorious hothead, by saying, "Make yourself at home, Frank—hit some-body." Sinatra laughed, and stars have lined up, hoping to be his next target, ever since.

Celebs with Comebacks

Henry Clay: "I would rather be right than be president." Congressman Reed: "He doesn't have to worry. He'll never be either."

———•◦•———

Lord Sandwich: "Really, Mr. Wilkes, I don't know whether you'll die on the gallows or of the pox." John Wilkes: "That will depend, my lord, on whether I embrace your principles or your mistress."

———•◦•———

Bessie Braddock: "Mr. Churchill, you are drunk!" Winston Churchill: "Yes, madam, and you are ugly. But in the morning, I will be sober."

———•◦•———

Nancy Astor: "Winston, if you were my husband, I'd put poison in your coffee." Winston Churchill: "Nancy, if you were my wife, I'd drink it."

Joe Frazier: "He's phony, using his blackness to get his way." Muhammad Ali: "Joe Frazier is so ugly he should donate his face to the U.S. Bureau of Wildlife."

Noel Coward: "You look almost like a man." Edna Ferber: "So do you."

Young man: "I can't bear fools." Dorothy Parker: "Apparently, your mother could."

Clare Boothe Luce: "Age before beauty." Dorothy Parker: "Pearls before swine."

"I've been called worse things by better men." —Pierre Trudeau's response to learning that Richard Nixon had called him an asshole

"Were you not breast-fed?"